Welcome to Russia

By Elma Schemenauer

The Child's World®

Published by The Child's World®
1980 Lookout Drive
Mankato, MN 56003-1705
800-599-READ
www.childsworld.com

Content Adviser: Kathleen Parthe, Ph.D., Director of Russian Studies,
University of Rochester, Rochester, NY
Design and Production: The Creative Spark, San Juan Capistrano, CA
Editorial: Publisher's Diner, Wendy Mead, Greenwich, CT
Photo Research: Deborah Goodsite, Califon, NJ

Cover and title page: Yoshio Tomii/SuperStock
Interior photos: Alamy: 14 (Bill Bachmann), 25 (Iain Masterton); AP Photo: 11 (file), 12 (Ivan
Sekretarev), 27 (Mikhail Metzel); Corbis: 10 (Bettmann), 13 (Antoine Gyori/Sygma); iStockphoto.com:
23 (Alain Couillaud), 28 (Ufuk Zivana), 29 (Cornel Stefan Achirei), 30 (Zastavkin), 31 (Isabelle
Mory); Landov: 3, 8 (Bryan & Cherry Alexander/Photoshot), 17 (Vladimir Zinin/ITAR-TASS), 19
(Vitaly Belousov/ITAR-TASS), 20 left (Anton Tushin/ITAR-TASS), 20 right (Alexander Kolbasov/
ITAR-TASS), 21 (Maxim Shipenkov/ITAR-TASS), 22 (Mikhail Fomichev/ITAR-TASS), 24 (Vitaly
Belousov/ITAR-TASS), 3, 26 (Viktor Korotayev/Reuters); Minden Pictures: 7 bottom (Konstantin
Mikhailov/Foto Natura), 9 (Konrad Wothe); NASA Earth Observatory: 4 (Reto Stockli); Oxford
Scientific: 7 top (Tony Waltham), 15 (Geoff Renner/Robert Harding Picture Library Ltd), 3, 16
(Gavrilov/Mauritius Die Bildagentur Gmbh); SuperStock: 6 (Jon Arnold Images).
Map: XNR Productions: 5

Library of Congress Cataloging-in-Publication Data
Schemenauer, Elma.
  Welcome to Russia / by Elma Schemenauer.
      p. cm. — (Welcome to the world)
  Includes index.
  ISBN-13: 978-1-59296-921-0 (library bound : alk. paper)
  ISBN-10: 1-59296-921-6 (library bound : alk. paper)
  1. Russia (Federation)—Juvenile literature. 2. Russia (Federation)—Social life and
customs—Juvenile literature. I. Title. II. Series.

DK510.76.S34 2007
947—dc22

2007005660

Contents

Where Is Russia?

What if you were a space traveler looking down on Earth? You would see huge land areas with water around them. These land areas are called **continents.** Some continents are made up of several countries. Russia covers large parts of two continents, Europe and Asia.

In the west, Russia borders European lands including Finland and Ukraine. In the south, it borders Asian lands including Mongolia and China. Oceans are on two sides of Russia. On the east is the Pacific Ocean. On the north is the cold Arctic Ocean.

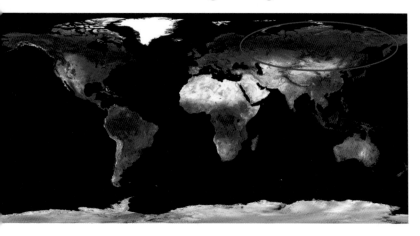

This picture gives us a flat look at Earth. Russia can be found inside the red circle.

Did you know?

Russia has a long name—"The Russian Federation." Many people just say "Russia" for short.

RUSSIA

★ National capital
● Other city

0   250   500 miles
0   250   500 kilometers

ARCTIC OCEAN

Wrangel Island

Bering Sea

UNITED STATES

Franz Josef Land

N
W   E
S

New Siberian Islands

Severnaya Zemlya

Novaya Zemlya

FINLAND

● Murmansk

aliningrad

St. Petersburg

● Arkhangel'sk

E U R O P E

Sea of Okhotsk

⊛ Moscow

● Nizhniy Novgorod

U R A L   M O U N T A I N S

● Yekaterinburg

Sakhalin Island

Lake Baikal

● Novosibirsk

CHINA

A   S   I   A

● Vladivostok

Caspian Sea

lack ea

KAZAKHSTAN

MONGOLIA

CHINA

CHINA

The Land

Flat plains called **steppes** cover much of Russia. Some steppe areas look like the flat farmlands of Kansas and Nebraska. Russia has mountains, too. The big ones are mostly in the south and east. The *Urals* are smaller.

Horses roam on one of Russia's many steppes.

They divide the country into two parts—*European Russia* and *Asian Russia.*

West of the Urals is European Russia. Many cities and towns can be found there. East of the Urals is Asian Russia, which is also called Siberia. Fewer people live here, and there are more open spaces. Lake Baikal, the deepest lake in the world, is found in Siberia. It is full of creatures that aren't found anywhere else.

Koryaksky volcano in Siberia

Lake Baikal

7

Reindeer in western Siberia

Plants and Animals

Farmers' fields cover many of Russia's flat, treeless steppes. The steppes are home to rabbits and other small animals. North of the steppes are thick forests with trees such as maples and pines. Here deer and lynxes hunt and sleep.

In the deep forests of the north, foxes, wolves, bears, and wild pigs live. Still farther north, only wildflowers, mosses, and small shrubs can be found. That is because it is Russia's Arctic area. It is very cold there. Only winter animals such as reindeer, polar bears, and seals are known to make their homes there.

Did you know?

The world's biggest cats are Siberian tigers, and they live in eastern Russia. They are very rare. In fact, only a few hundred are left in the wild. Russians are working to make sure these giant cats do not die out.

8

Siberian tigers can weigh more than 600 pounds (272 kilograms).

This is an illustration of the Viking leader Rurik.

Long Ago

About 1,600 years ago, a group of people called the Slavs came to what is now Russia. Years later, a Viking chief named Rurik set up a government there. Rurik and other rulers were very powerful. They ruled over many people in lots of different areas. As time went on, Russian leaders called **czars** ruled over the people and lands. The most powerful of these rulers were named Ivan, Peter, Catherine, Nicholas, and Alexander.

Many people did not like the czars. Under their leadership, lots of people were poor and unhappy. In 1917, a group of mostly poor people started a **revolution** against the czars. They set up a new government. It ruled by **communist** ideas. This meant people could not run their own businesses. The government ran the businesses. People could not own land or homes. The government owned them. But many did not think communist rule worked well. In 1991 it fell apart.

Vladimir Lenin (center) helped create Russia's communist government in 1917.

A Russian woman casts her vote.

Russia Today

Now, for the first time, Russia has a democratic government. People vote to decide who their leaders will be. Also, the government no longer controls everything. This means Russians are changing. They are running their own businesses. They are farming for themselves, not for the government. They are using the Internet to learn new ideas.

The changes have not been easy. Without government controls, prices have gone up. Workers sometimes have to work for months without being paid. Some Russians think life was better before communist rule fell apart. Some think a democratic government is better because they can make more choices about how to live and what to do.

Since the end of communism, people sometimes have to pay more for food and other goods.

The People

Russia has about 145 million people. Most live in the European part of the country. Many Russians are **descendants** of the Slavs who arrived 1,600 years ago. But there are also

People walk around Red Square in Moscow.

people of many other backgrounds. These include Jews, Germans, and Armenians. Some Russians are Bashkirs, who come from the country of Turkey. Others are Tatars, who have relatives in Turkey and the country of Mongolia.

Many native peoples live in Russia, including Eskimos in the far eastern part of the country.

Moscow is one of Russia's biggest and busiest cities.

City Life and Country Life

Two women work on their garden at their dacha.

Most Russians live in cities, which are often crowded. For most city people, home is a small apartment in a tall building. Grandparents often live with the family. Many city people have a summer home, or **dacha** (DA-chah), so they can get away from the city for a while. A dacha may be a large house in the country, or it may be a tiny cottage with a small garden on the edge of the city.

In the country, life is less crowded. But people living far from cities may not have electricity, cars, or running water. Most live in houses or apartments. They travel on trains and buses, which go almost everywhere and stop often.

Did you know?

St. Petersburg was Russia's capital for 200 years. Russians are very proud of it and still call it their "northern capital."

Schools and Language

Most Russian children go to kindergarten, and all have to attend school from ages 6 to 17. Among subjects studied are reading, writing, science, math, history, English, and music. When school begins on September 1, students bring flowers to their teachers. Their families come to join in celebrating the new school year.

Soon after Russia became a country, people from the country of Greece worked out a way to write the Russian language. One of these people was called Cyril (SEE-rill) so the alphabet is called **Cyrillic** (Suh-RILL-ik). Today Russians still use the alphabet the Greeks made for them. Besides Russian, people speak many other languages such as German, Armenian, Ukrainian, and Tatar.

ГОРОДСКАЯ СИМВОЛИКА

1 СЕНТЯБРЯ.
ЗДРАВСТВУЙ
ШКОЛА !!

**Students gather in a Moscow classroom
to celebrate the first day of school.**

Work

Many Russian city people work in offices, stores, factories, and hospitals. In many families both the father and the mother work outside the home. A lot of doctors and teachers are women. So are many street sweepers.

In the country, many of the people farm crops or fish in the seas for food to sell. Some country people are miners, since Russia has lots of minerals such as coal, iron, copper, and tin. Some people work with oil and natural gas, since Russia has plenty of these, too.

A miner shovels coal in a mine in Kisilyovsk.

A Russian family has tea together.

Food

Russians love soup. In fact, many people think that you will stay healthy if you eat at least one bowl of soup a day! Russian soups, often served with black bread, include cabbage soup and a type of beet soup called **borscht**

A bowl of borscht

(BORSHT). Many Russians grow their own cabbage, beets, potatoes, carrots, cucumbers, and other vegetables. City families do this at their dacha, or summer home.

Most Russians eat their main meal at noon. First they might have salad. After this they might eat fish or meat with potatoes. Dessert might be a sweet cream cake or cool slices of watermelon. Tea is a favorite drink in Russia.

Young girls at ballet class

Pastimes

Russians like to read, see movies, watch TV, play card games, and go to museums. Many young people take ballet lessons. Some also learn to play the guitar.

Like many other countries, soccer is a favorite pastime in Russia. But ice hockey is a favorite team sport, too. In fact, Russian ice hockey players are famous around the world! Among other popular sports in Russia are hiking, skiing, swimming, skating, and gymnastics.

Did you know?

Russia has more than 50,000 public libraries. Russians can find more than a billion books to read!

A boy guards the goal during an ice hockey game.

Holidays

Are you used to Christmas being on December 25? In Russia it is on January 7. This is because Russia's main religious group, the Russian Orthodox Church, uses an older calendar than most Americans do. It is called the Julian calendar.

These girls light candles as part of their Christmas celebration.

Russia also has many non-religious holidays. One is Soldier's Day on February 23. It is a holiday for all men, not just soldiers. Another is Women's Day on March 8. A favorite holiday in Russia is New Year's Day. Some people like New Year's so much that they celebrate it twice, once on January 1 and again on January 14!

Thousands of people gather to celebrate the start of the New Year in Moscow.

Russia is a country that has gone through many changes. It is building its future while honoring its past. If you ever get a chance to go to Russia, you can learn more about this nation's fascinating history and see its beautiful artwork by visiting one of its many museums.

27

Fast Facts About Russia

Area: About 10.7 million square miles (17 million square miles). That's about twice the size of the United States.

Population: 145 million people.

Capital City: Moscow.

Other Important Cities: St. Petersburg, Nizhniy Novgorod, Novosibirsk, Yekaterinburg.

Money: The ruble. A ruble is divided into 100 kopecks.

National Flag: The flag has three sideways stripes. Colors from top to bottom are white, blue, and red.

National Animal: The bear.

National Holiday: Russia Day on June 12.

Head of Government: The prime minister.

Head of State: The president.

National Song:
"The Russian National Anthem"

Russia, our holy country!
Russia, our beloved country!
A mighty will, a great glory,
Are your inheritance for all time!

Be glorious, our free Fatherland!
Eternal union of fraternal peoples,
Common wisdom given by our forebears,
Be glorious, our country! We are proud of you!

From the southern seas to the polar region
Spread our forests and fields.
You are unique in the world, inimitable,
Native land protected by God!

Wide spaces for dreams and for living
Are opened for us by the coming years
Faithfulness to our country gives us strength
Thus it was, so it is and always will be!

Famous People:

Mikhail Baryshnikov: ballet dancer

Anton Chekhov: writer

Yuri Gagarin: Russian astronaut, first person in space

Mikhail Gorbachev: former leader of the Soviet Union

Anna Pavlova: ballet dancer

Alexander Pushkin: famous author

Vladimir Putin: president

Peter Ilich Tchaikosky: composer

Valentina Tereshkova: first woman in space

Leo Tolstoy: author

Russian Folklore:

Baba Yaga

Baba Yaga is a legendary witch who appears in many Russian folktales. She is known for her iron teeth and lives in a house with chicken legs that can move around. Baba Yaga flies through the air inside of a bowl called a mortar and uses a stick called a pestle to steer. She tries to capture people and make them her next meal. But, fortunately, her victims escape with help from Baba Yaga's own servants and animals. In some stories, she has two other sisters, also named Baba Yaga.

How Do You Say...

ENGLISH	RUSSIAN	HOW TO SAY IT
hello	zdrastvuytye	zdrast-VOO-yuh-tuh
goodbye	da svidaniya	da svee-DAH-nee-yah
please	pazhalusta	pah-ZHA-loo-stuh
thank you	spasiba	spa-SEE-bah
one	adin	ah-DIN
two	dva	DVAH
three	tri	TREE
Russia	Rasiya	roh-SEE-yah

Glossary

borscht (BORSHT) Borscht is a soup that is made with beets. Many Russians like to eat borscht.

communist (KOM-yoo-nist) Under a communist government, people do not own their businesses or homes. Instead the government runs things and makes decisions for the whole country.

continents (KON-tuh-nents) Most of the land areas on Earth are in huge sections called continents. Russia is on the continents of Europe and Asia.

Cyrillic (suh-RILL-ik) the Russian alphabet created by Cyril of Greece.

czars (ZARZ) Czars were people who ruled Russia long ago. Many people did not like how the czars ruled.

dacha (DA-chah) A dacha is a Russian's summer home. Dachas can be big or small.

descendants (di-SEND-uhnts) People who come from a common ancestor, or relative, are called descendants. Children would be considered the descendants of their parents, grandparents, and earlier generations.

revolution (rev-uh-LOO-shun) When people overthrow their rulers, it's called a revolution.

steppes (STEPS) Steppes are flat, treeless plains. Much of Russia is covered with steppes.

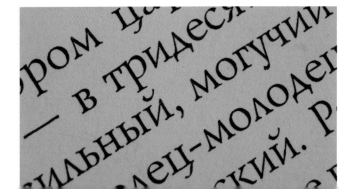

Further Information

Read It

Gray, Susan H. *Russia.* Minneapolis, MN: Compass Point Books, 2002.

Hintz, Martin. *Russia.* Danbury, CT: Children's Press, 2005.

Murrell, Kathleen Berton. *Russia.* New York: Dorling Kindersley, 2000.

Look It Up

Visit our Web page for lots of links about Russia:
http://www.childsworld.com/links

Note to Parents, Teachers, and Librarians: We routinely verify our Web links to make sure they are safe, active sites—so encourage your readers to check them out!

Index